Sacred Summer

Isabelle Athmann

ISBN 978-1-387-63399-9

dedication

to all those who have
grown wiser with the Summer...
this flourish Sacred

introduction

Again, I announce in a rhyming poetic construction the value of a season that I claim to be sacred and acknowledge a required treatise on the nature of Summer's temper. The seasonal rotation from Divine Spring marks the presence of the warming Sun, and this endowment fosters our most precious gifts, relished by all, the Sacred Summer months. The illustrations celebrate the value we grew to anticipate and continually enjoy. The Sacred Summer Sun feeds us all, for which I give thanks here as a poem to express my profound gratitude and joy for the combined warmth this summer season brings. Not to forget the petrichor experience when Summer rains nourish us all; fields, forests, and gardens are regarded and respected here. This credit to the Sacred Summer and her warm Sun is, in hope, duly noted in poetic moments and illustrations and can be seen as an invitation for considerable pleasing recognition and delight. In discovering all merits, this season's many miracles deserve such a treatise of profound appreciation, thereby documented here.

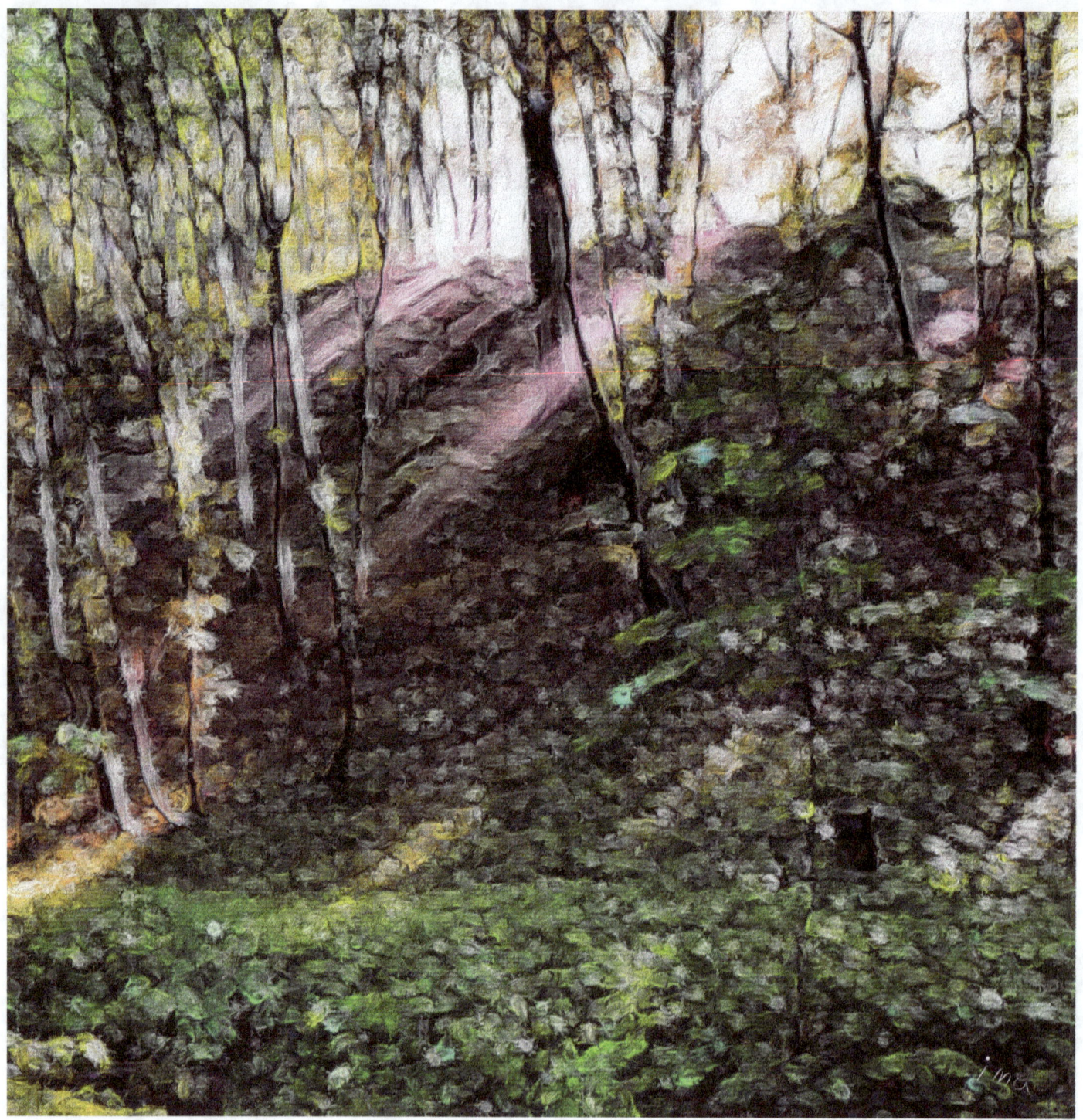

The Sacred Summer Sun, on the solstice,
ends our lingering saisonnière lunar chill woes.
Bringing warmth throughout the essential
cores, even down to roots and toes.

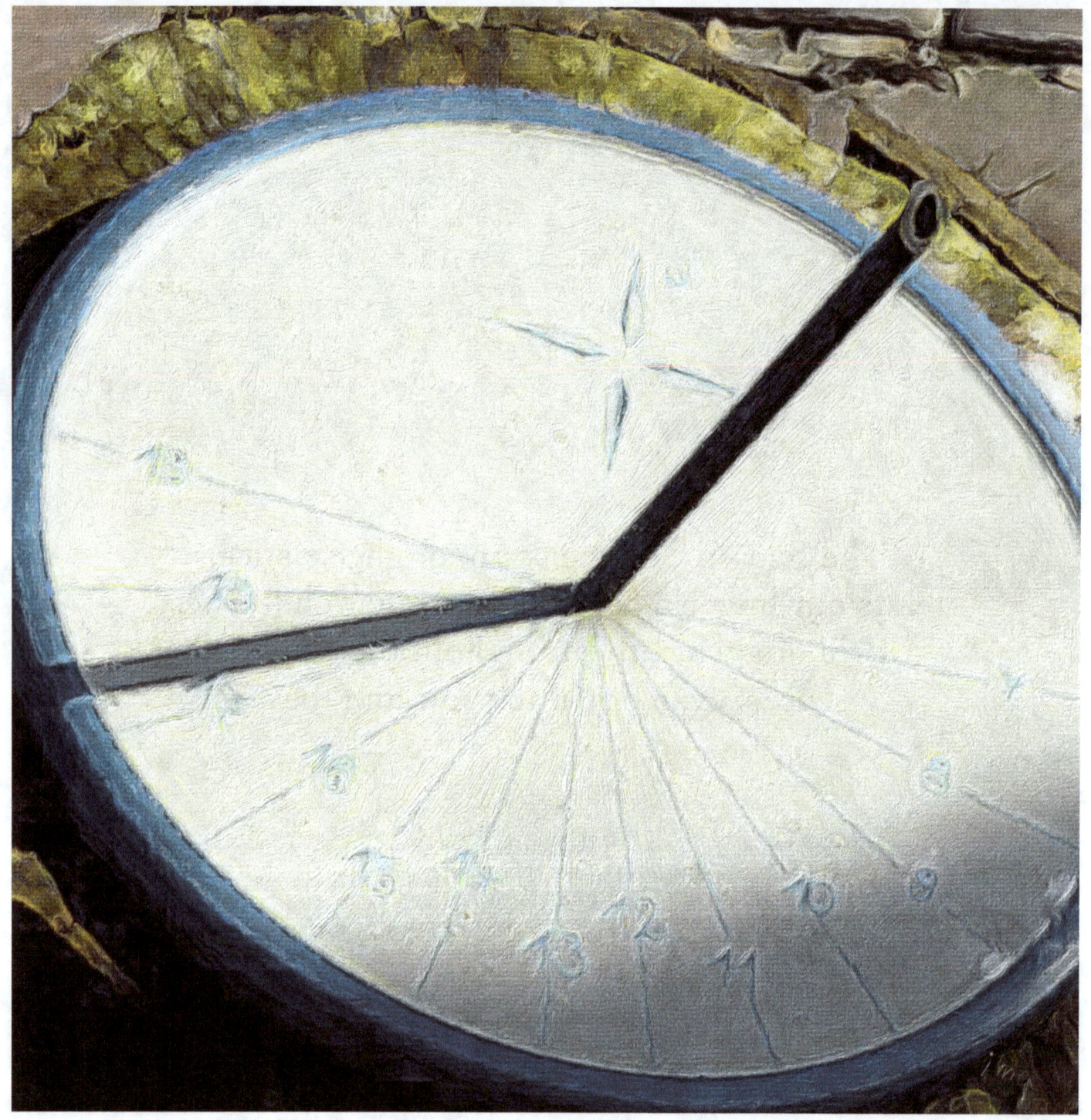

This ray of warmth forever increases through about three, and quelques jours, glorious months.

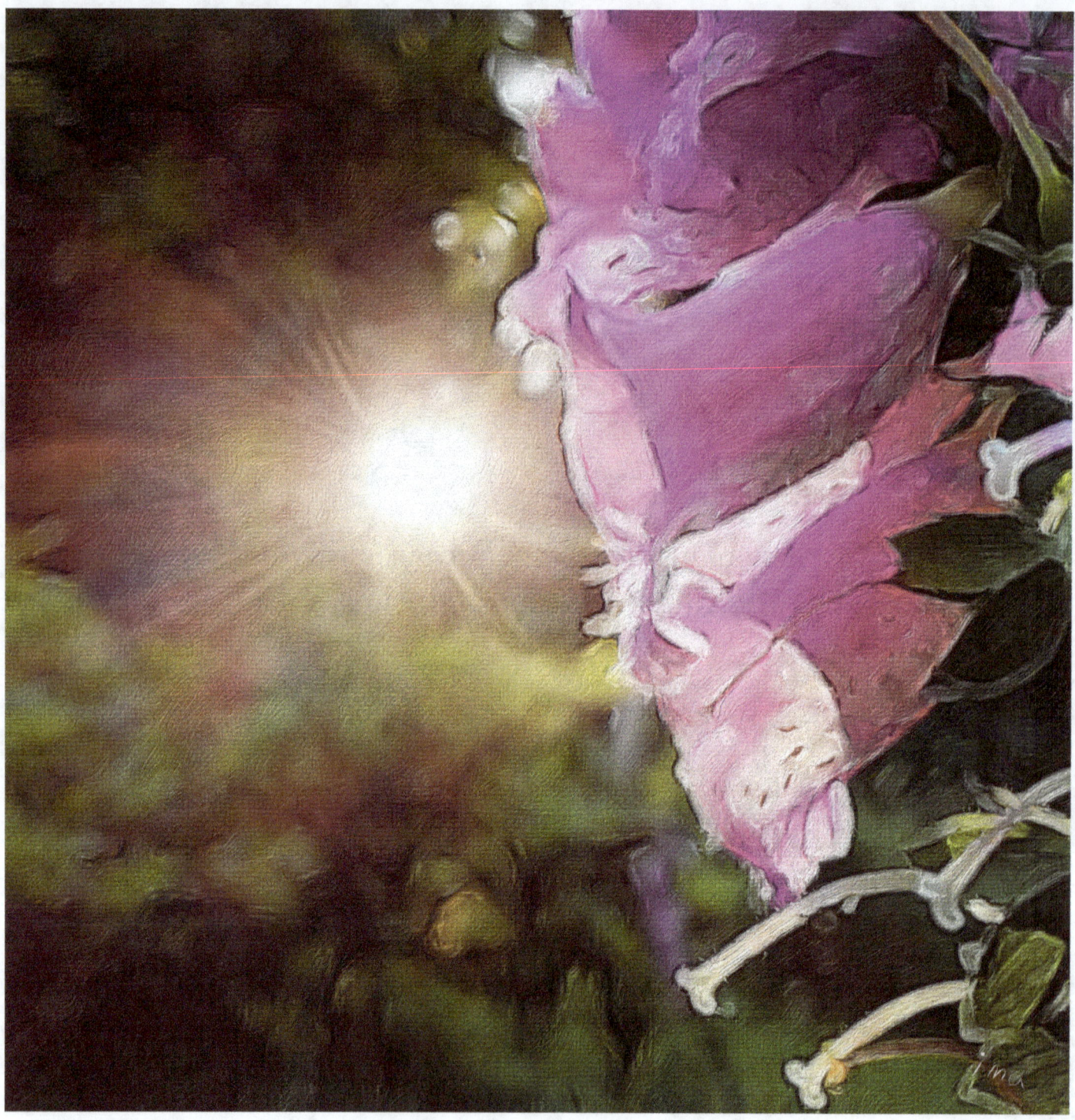

Forever gaining traction with this calm, curing, solacing, and earnestness punch.

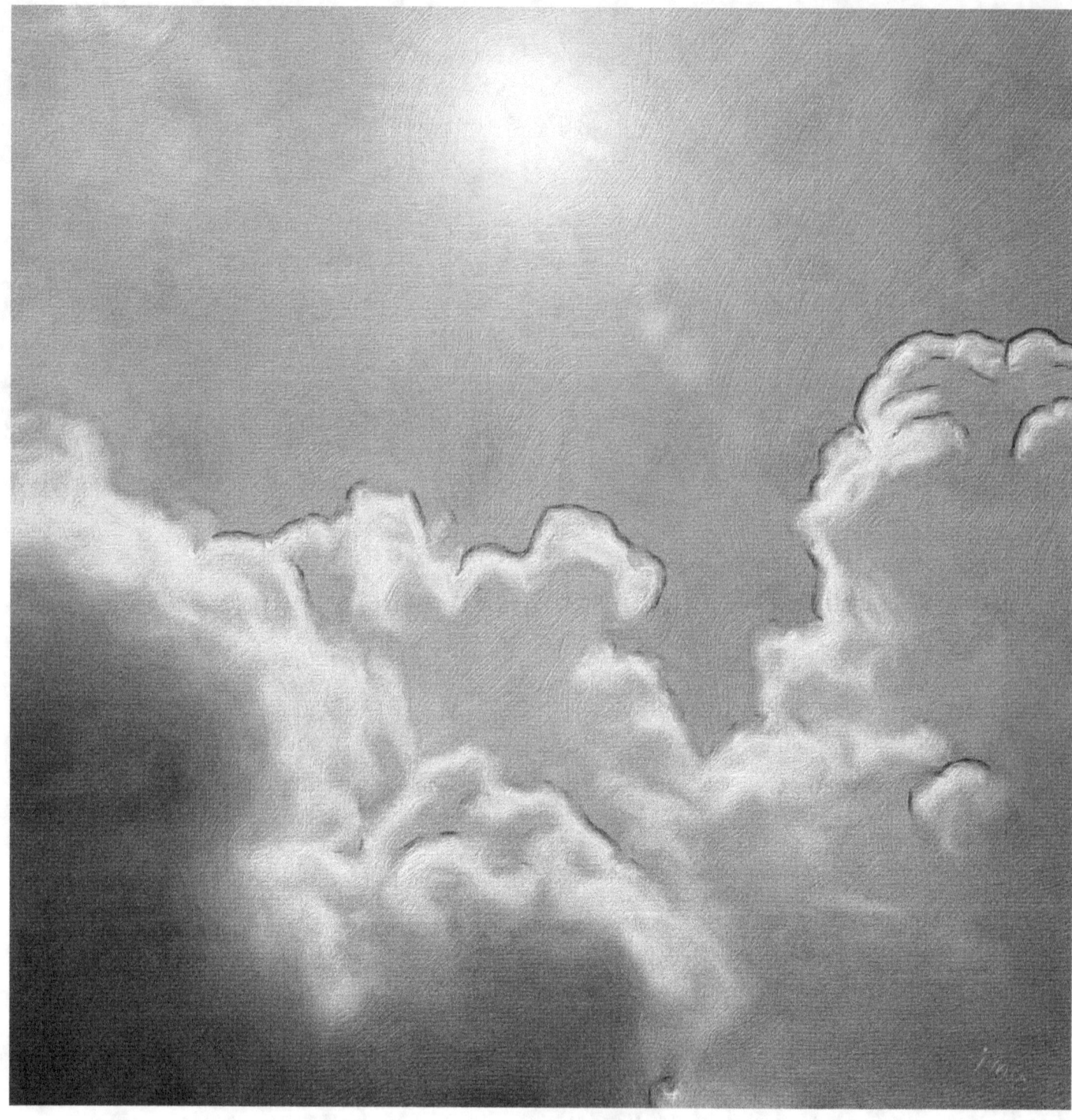

Like all seasons, the start of Summer's temper
is somewhere in the mid-middle.

◑ 21	22
Hear Ye! Hear Ye!	
Sacred Summer	
1st Day of Summer	
28	● 29

Encouraging our wall calendar's solstice
schedule to be very civil.

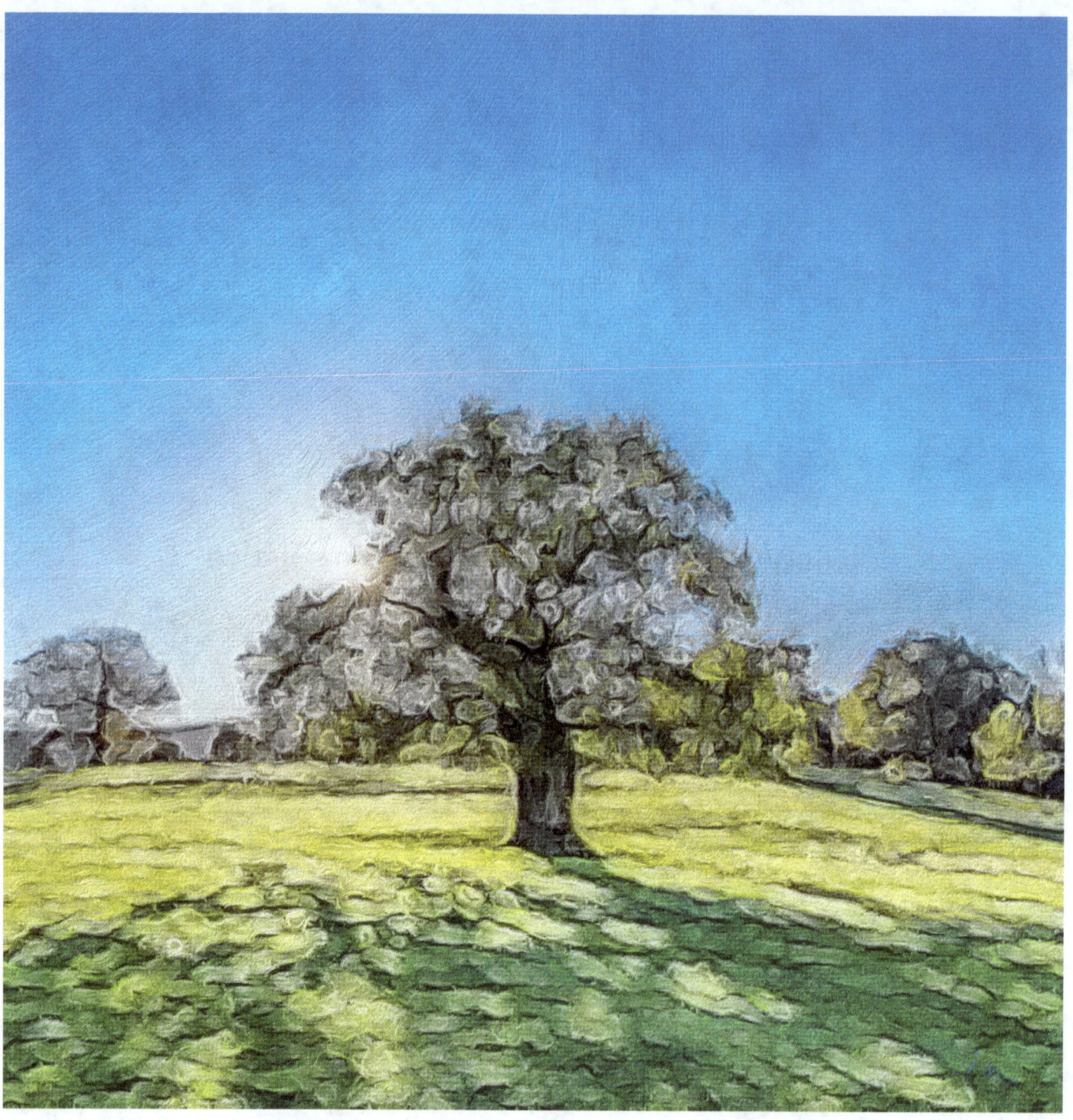

Marking the Summer Solstice Day divine and to all acknowledged... Hear Ye! Hear Ye! Sacred.

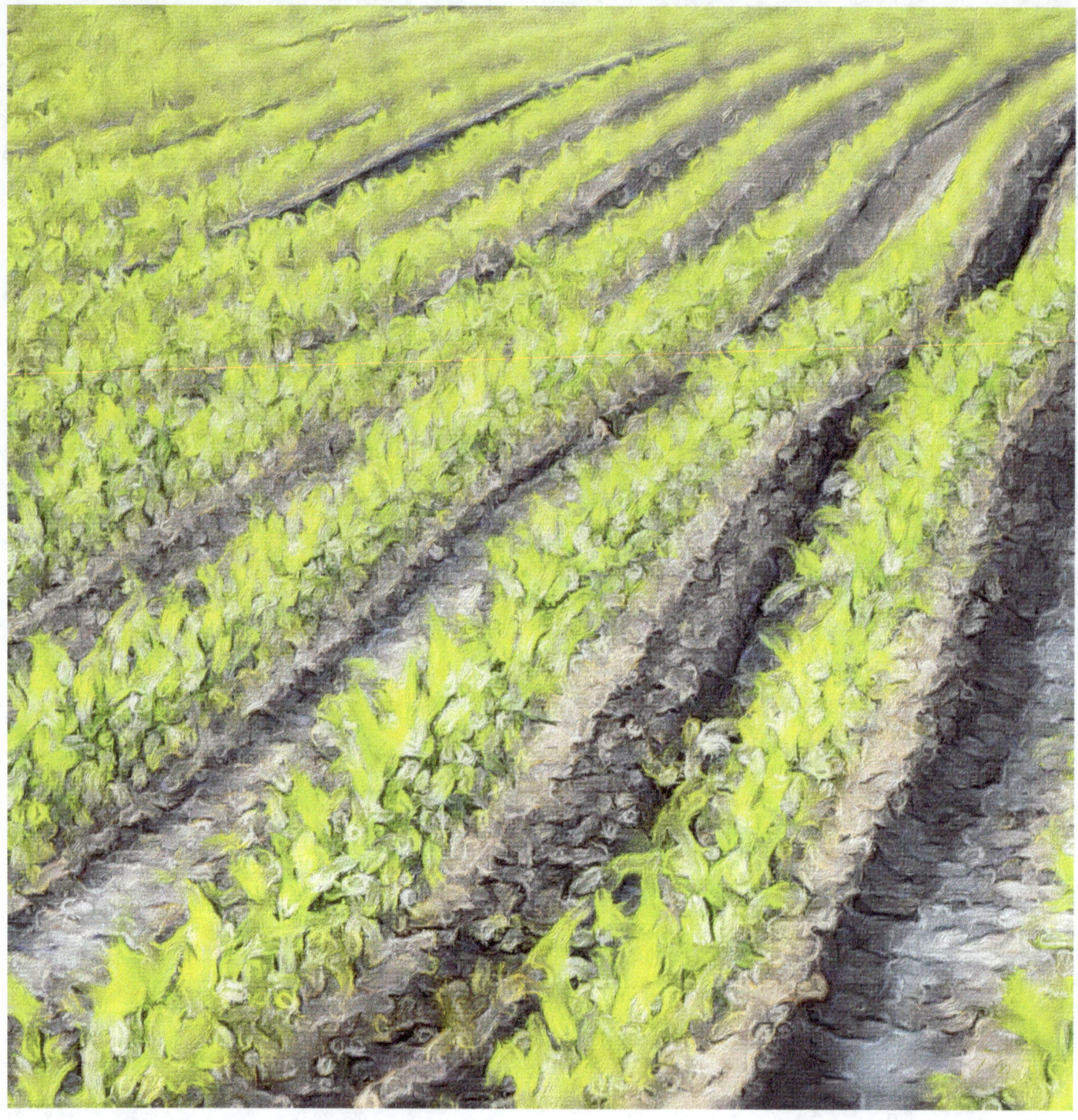

Improving every day on Divine Spring
and what the season's growth created.

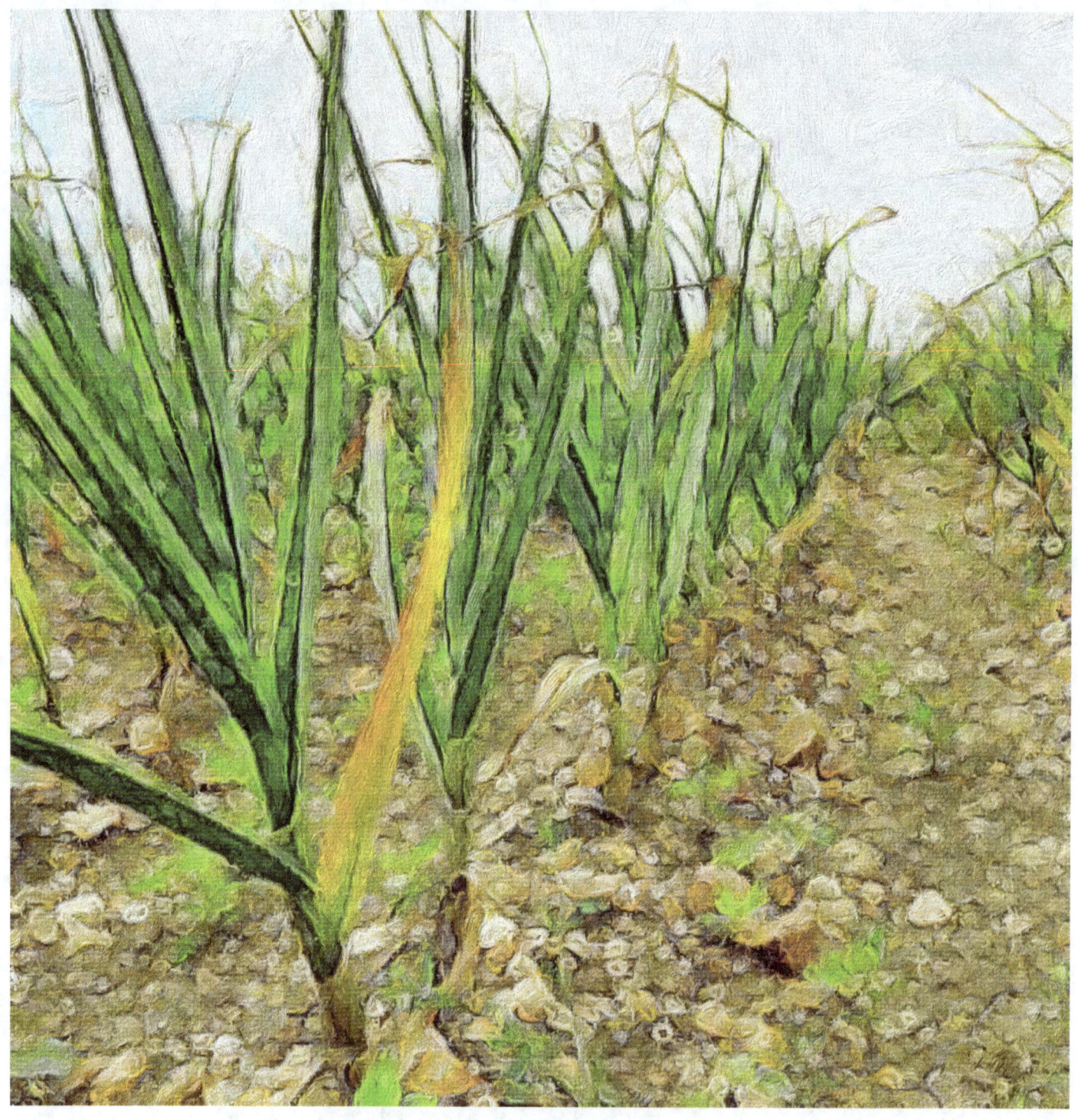

This eagerness for sincere Summer
warmth has deep, tender roots.
Growing in these temps très chaud, a pearl of courageous
wisdom shares the youthful fortitude already introduced..

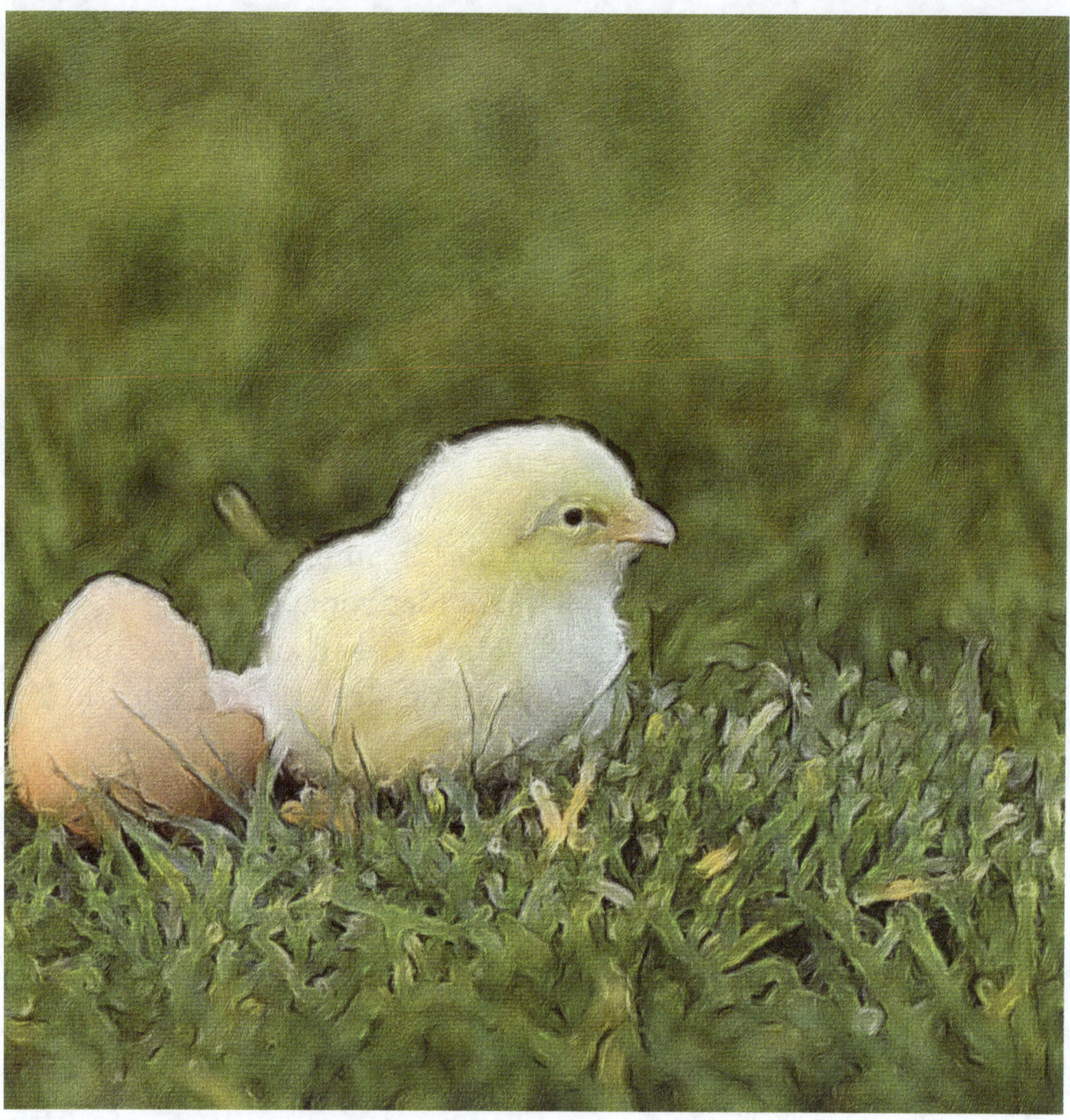

Hark to these altrical/precocial births
that began with Divine Spring.

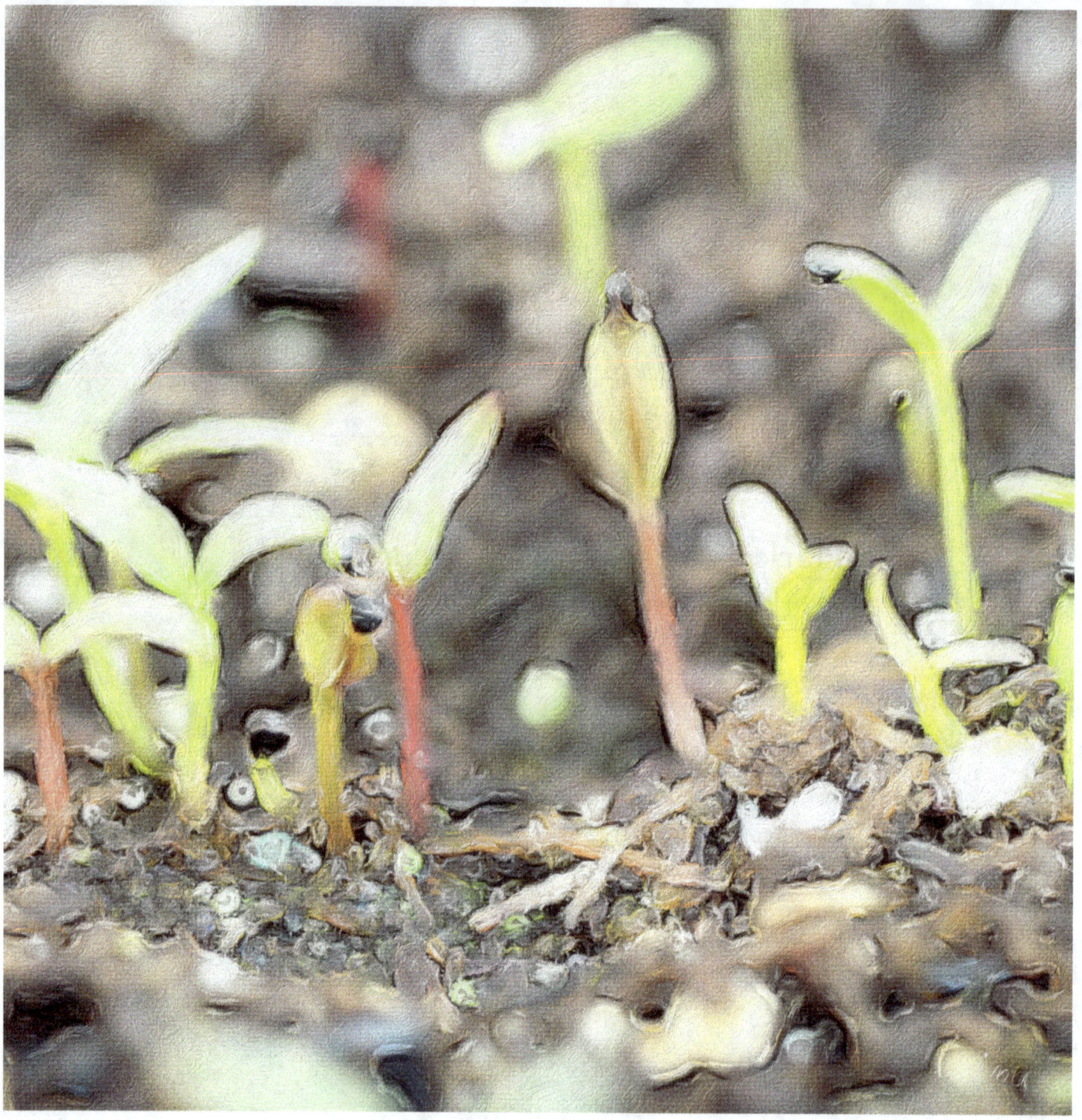

Sacred Summer speeds forth la croissance
des plantes germination upswing.

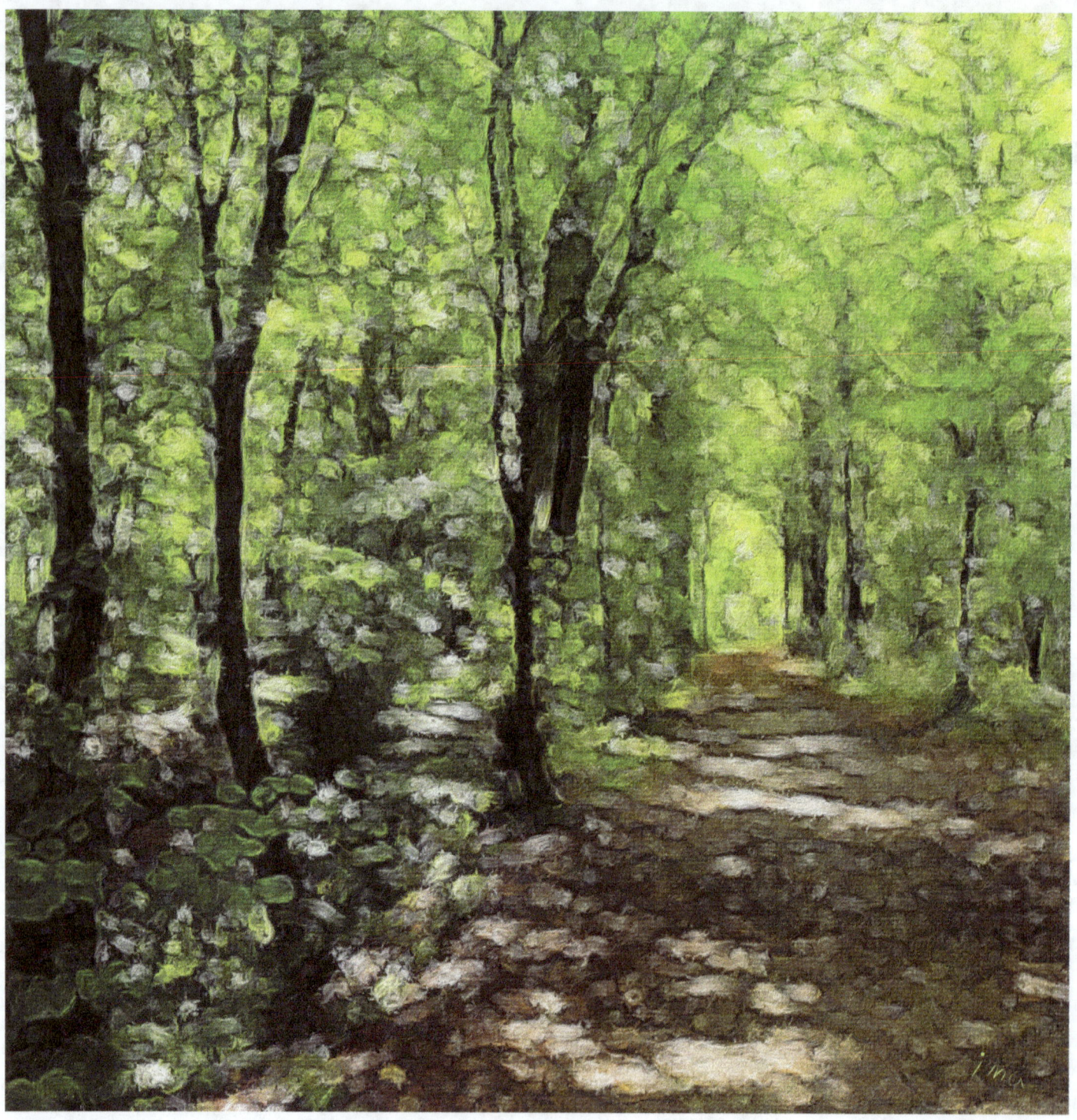

Thriving deciduous growth encourages spheres of joy.

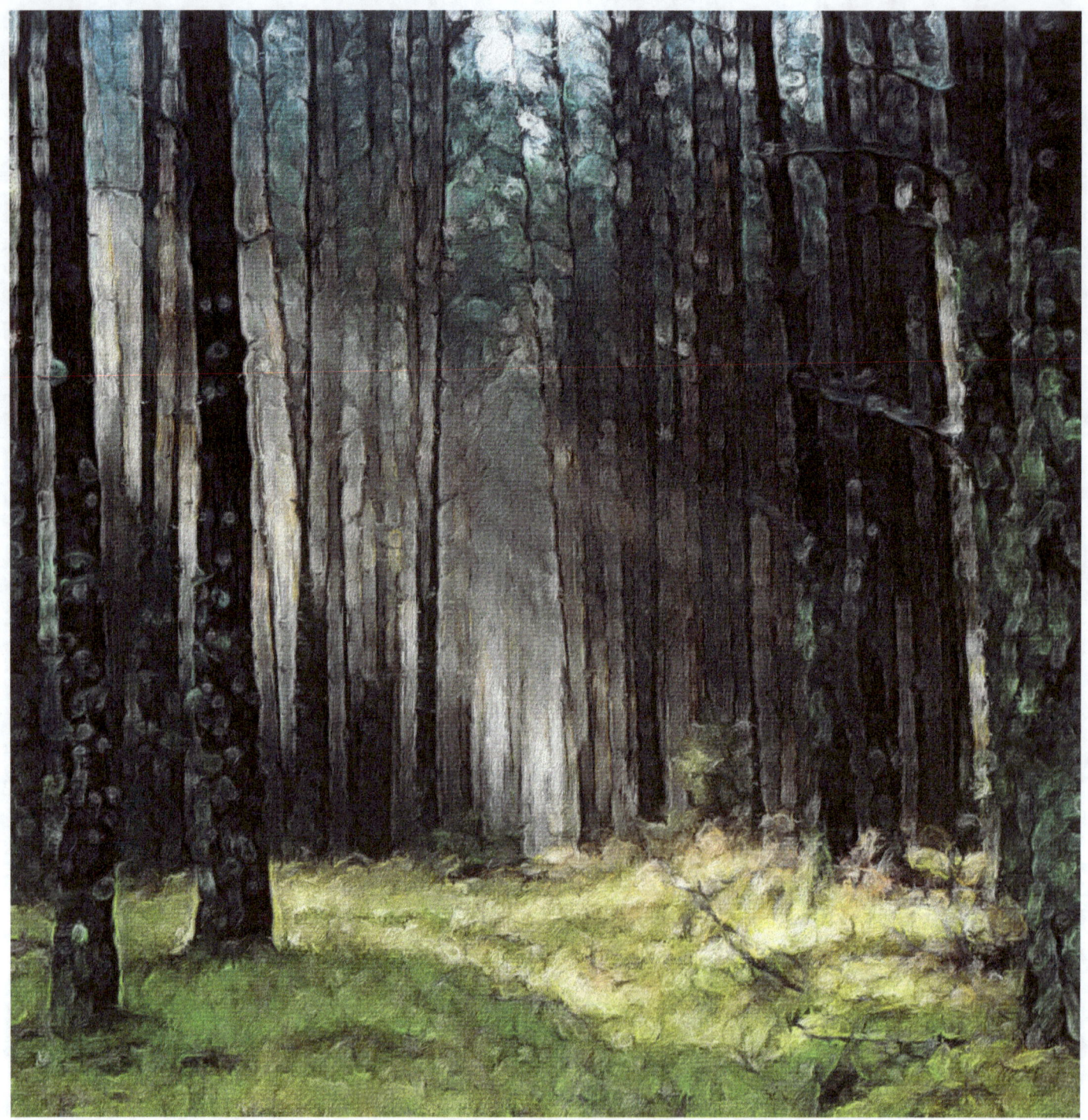

Reassured conifers relax and increase
their ever-flourishing voice.

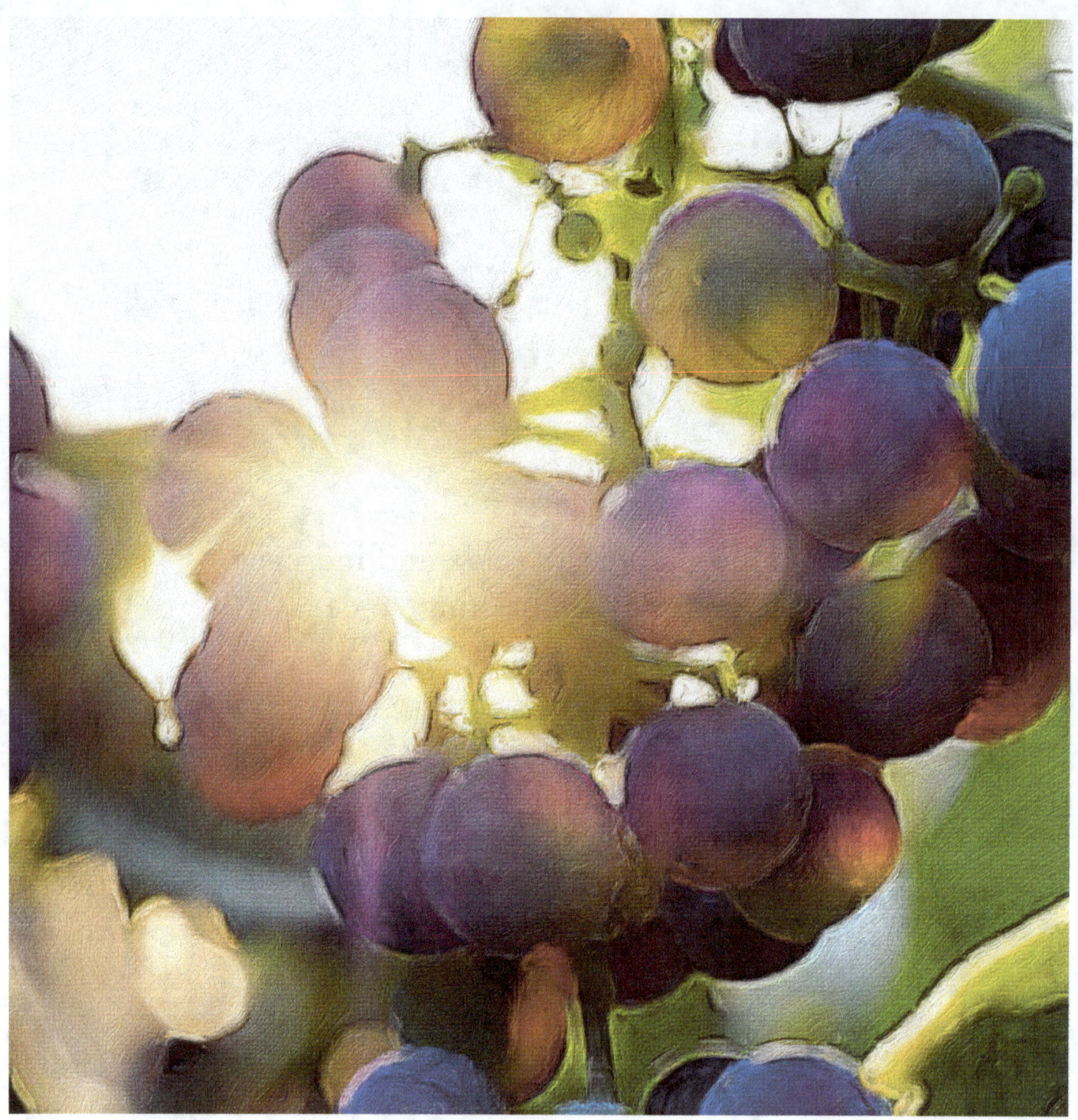

our Summer Sunbeams
are forever nourishing...
sacred sustenance

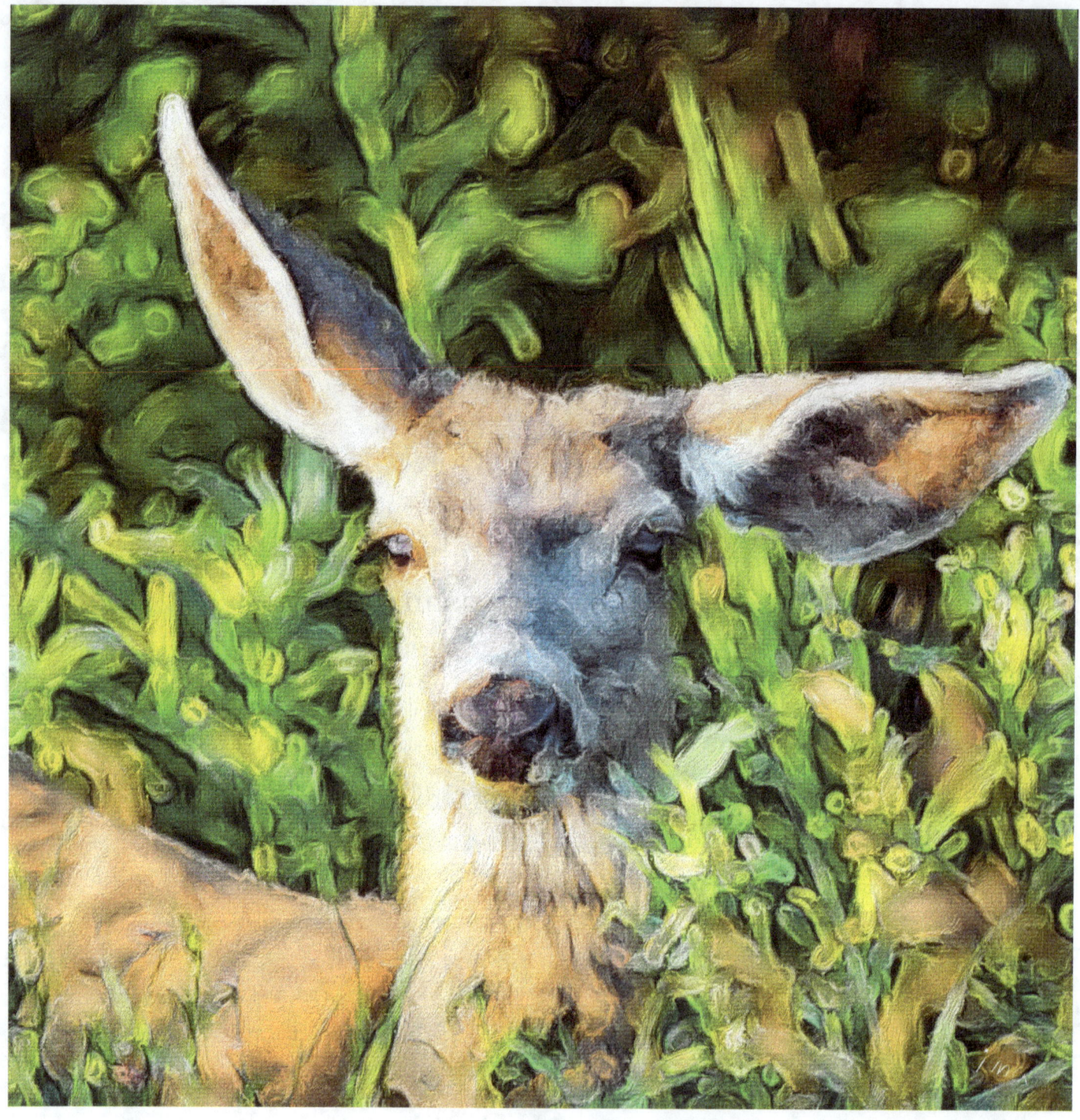

The advance of Sacred Summer months
thrives on retrieving generational wisdom.
And welcomes the same, God's wise animal kingdom.

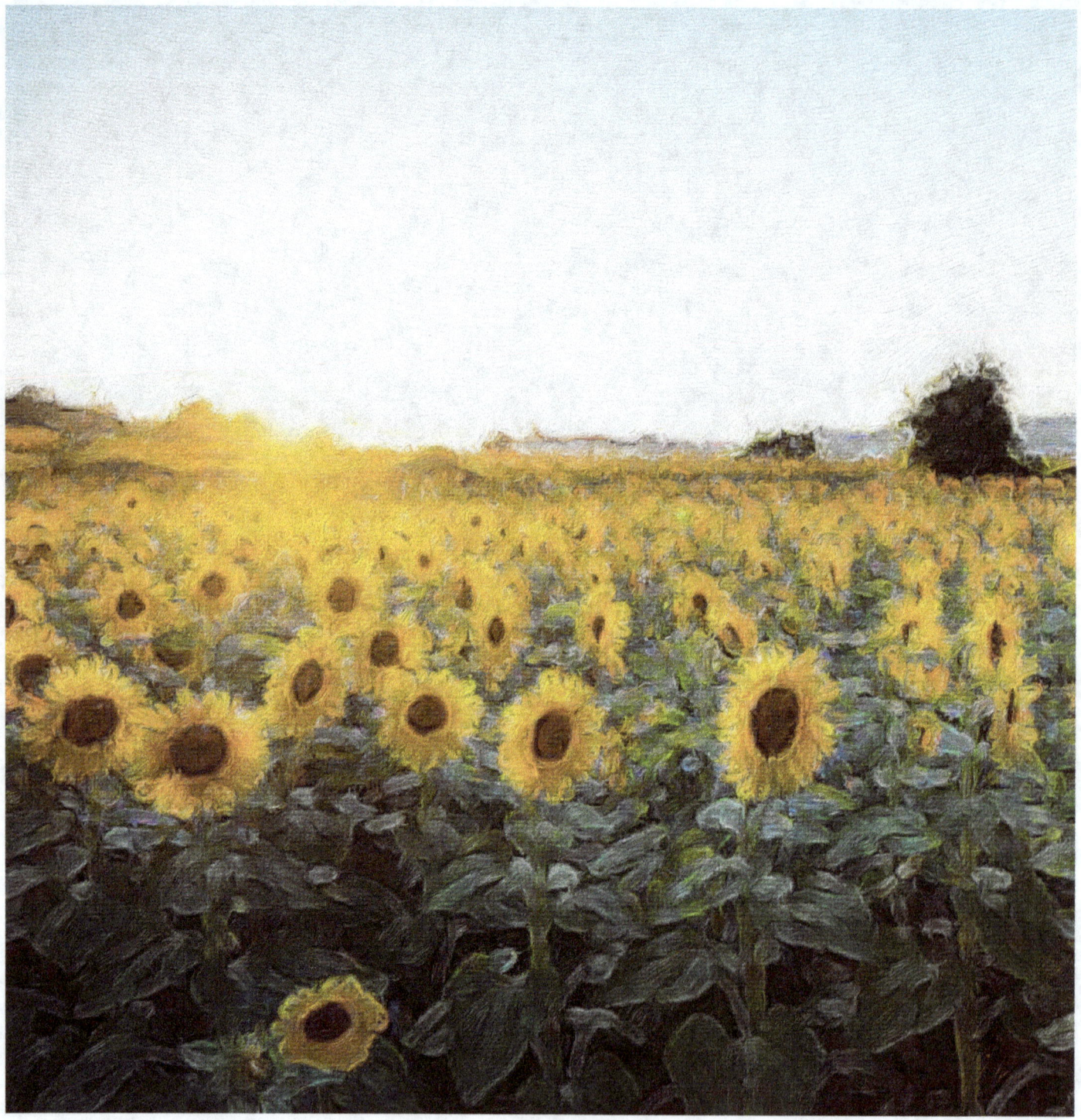

Are you, are you like I, eager for the fields of sunflowers?

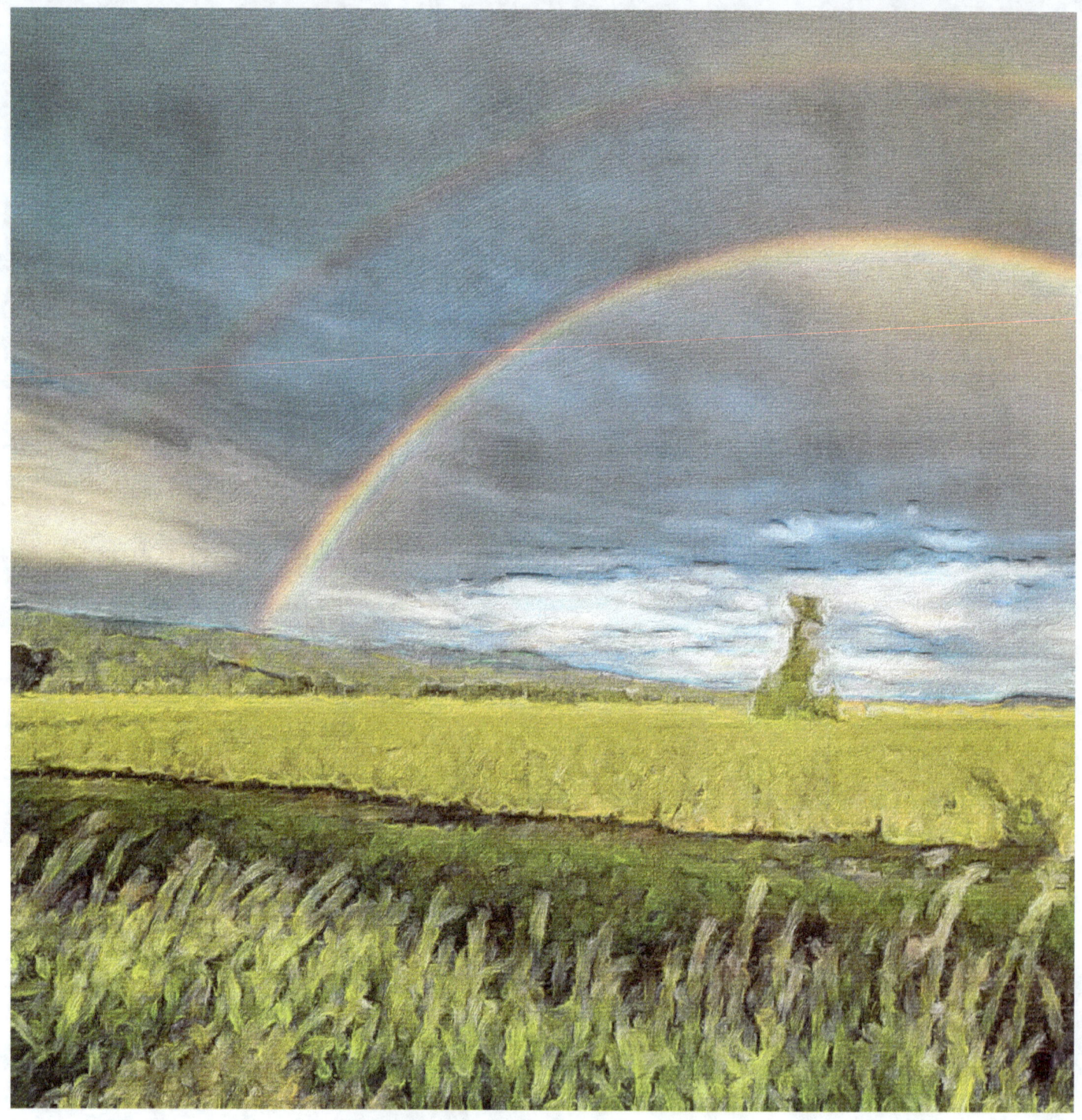

These welcoming mirrors mimic all her sunshowers.

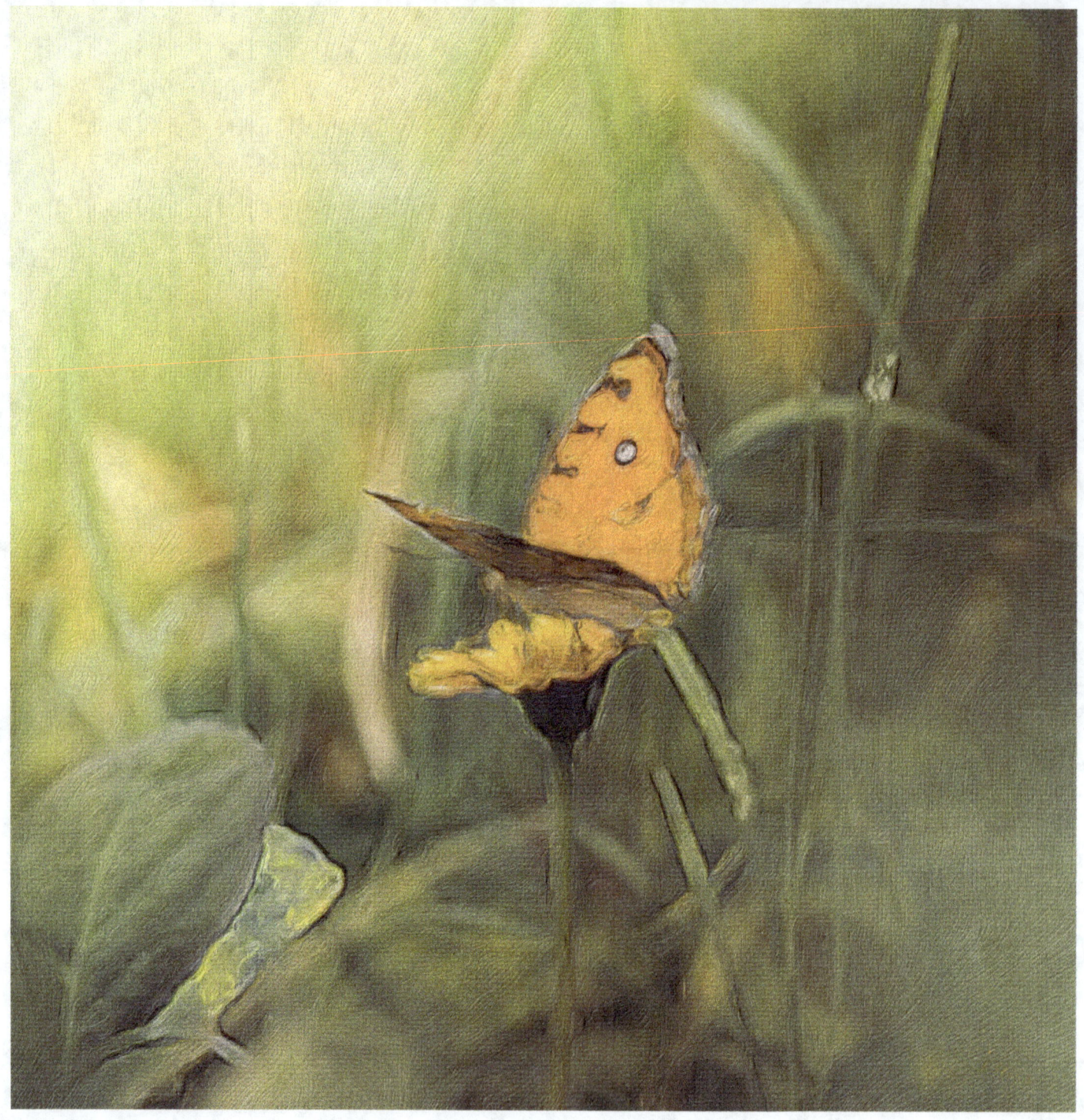

And indeed, note that the sacred butterflies increase our crops.

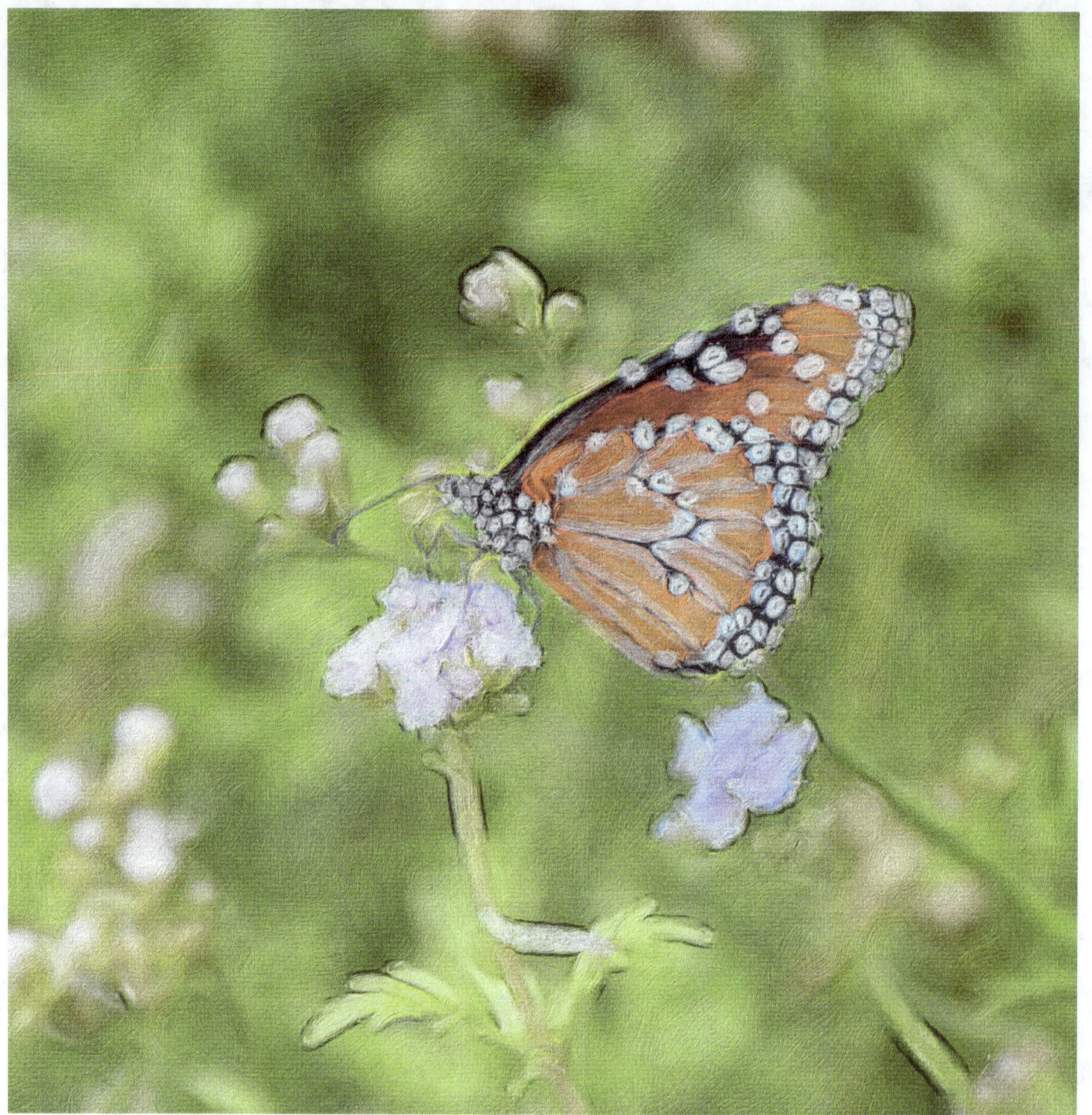

The Sacred Summer seasonal rotation
changes the rhythmic clocks.

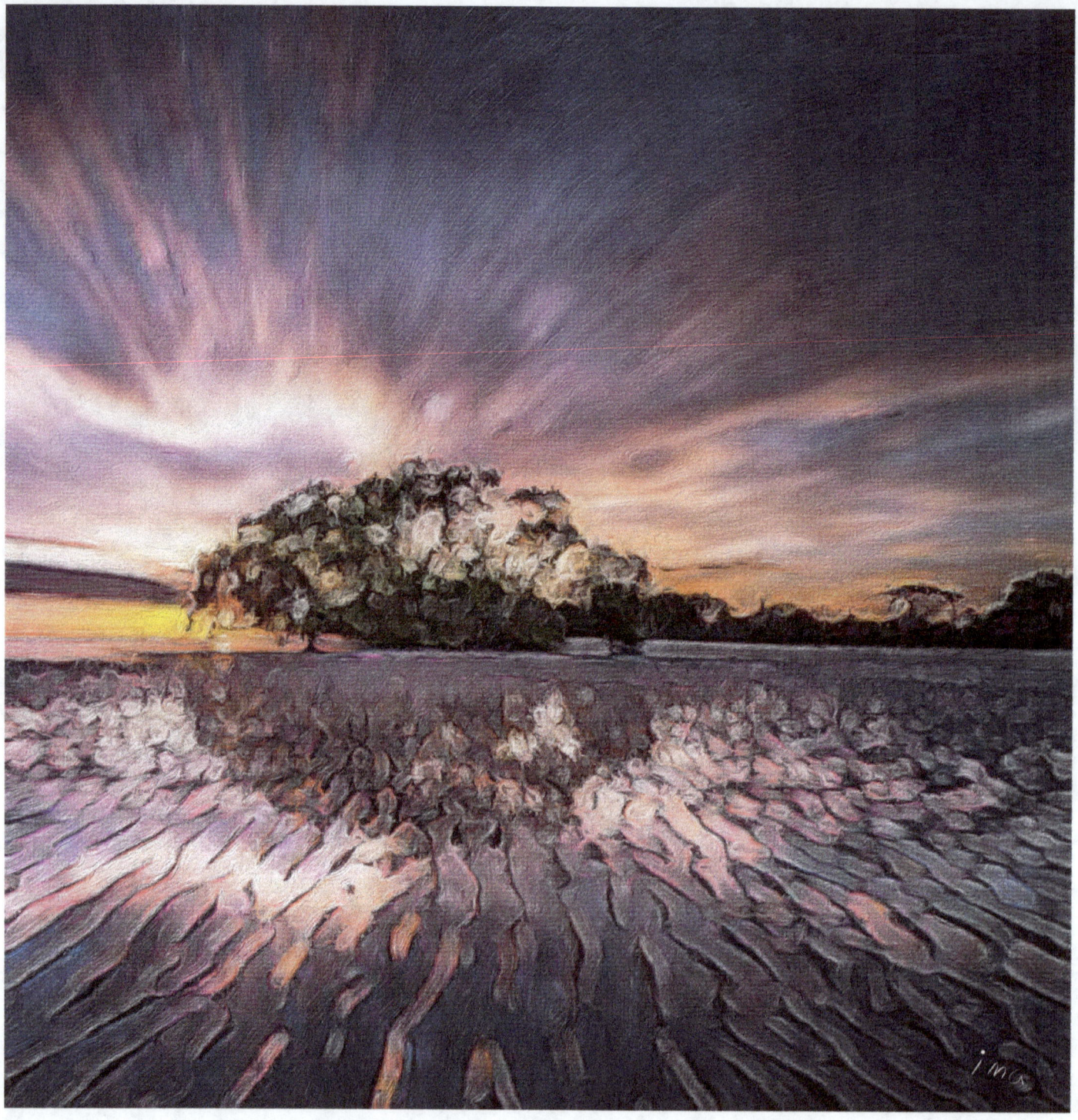

Sending mullers in contemplation to
glorious and spectacular beaches.

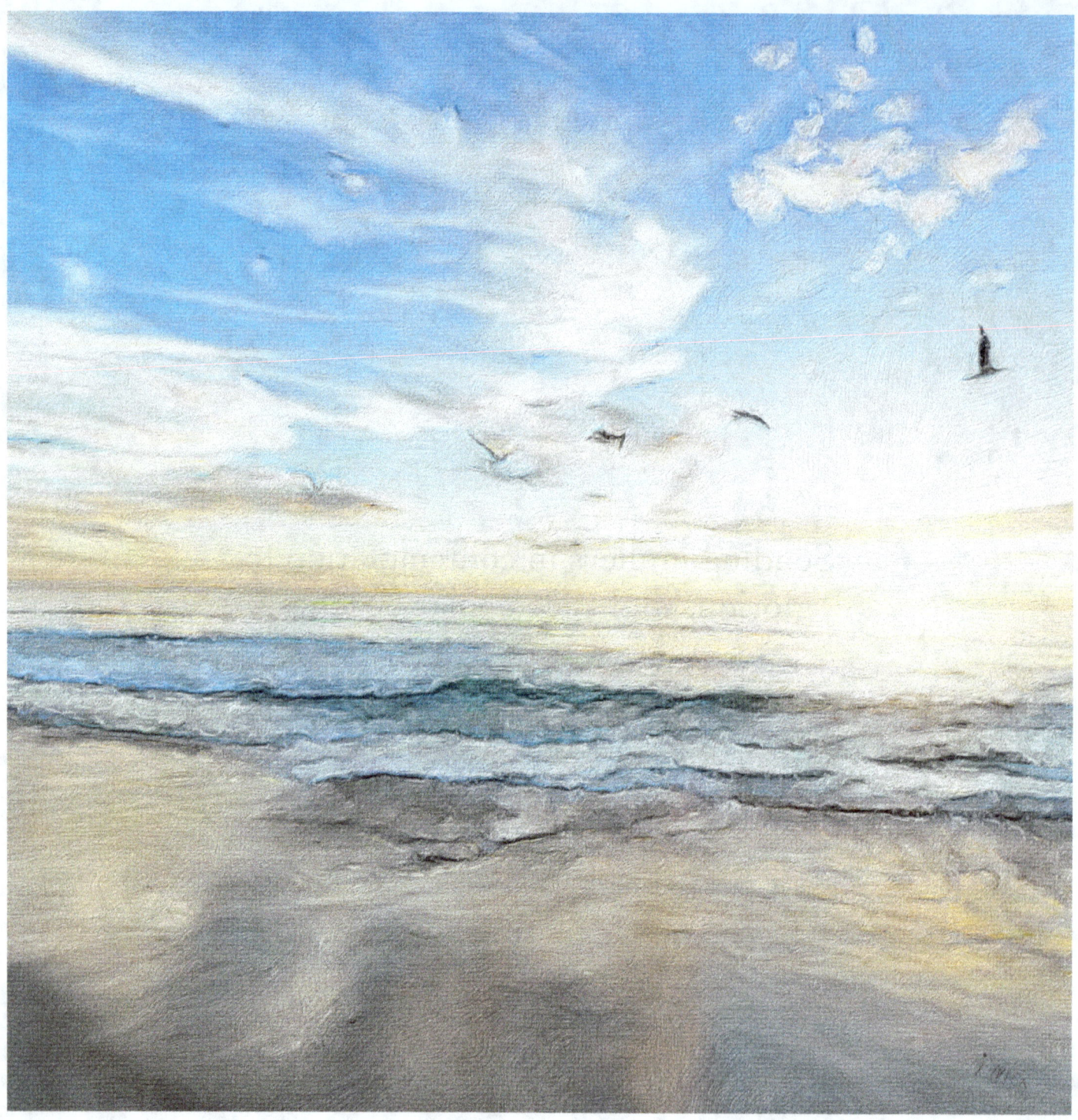

The latish setting Sun highlights a delightful
find - those precious flying creatures.

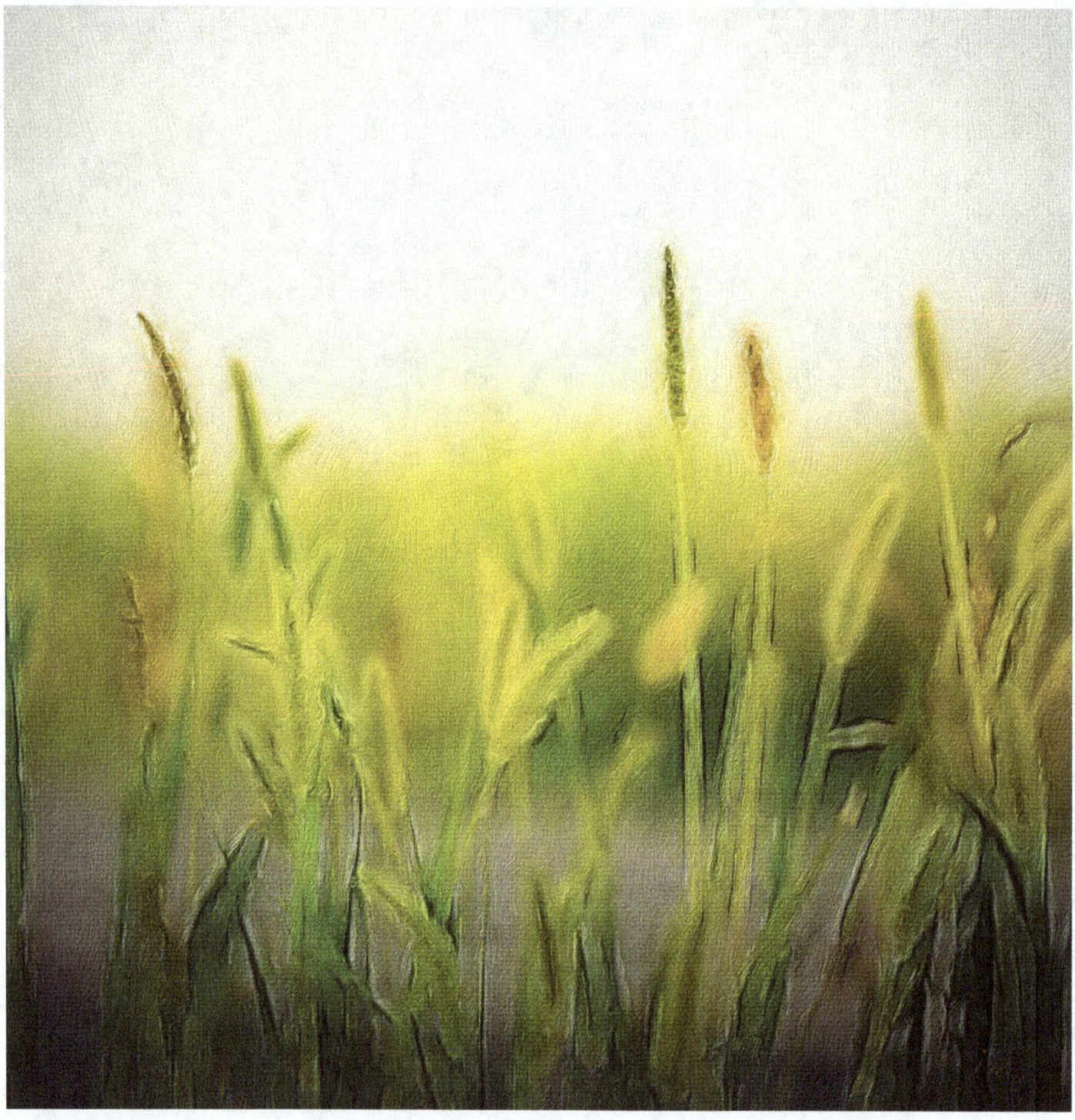

Fields of grain grow strong within,
do promise of goodwill bread.
The sacred Sun, to its core, her rays are the
land-to-farmer's goodness thread.

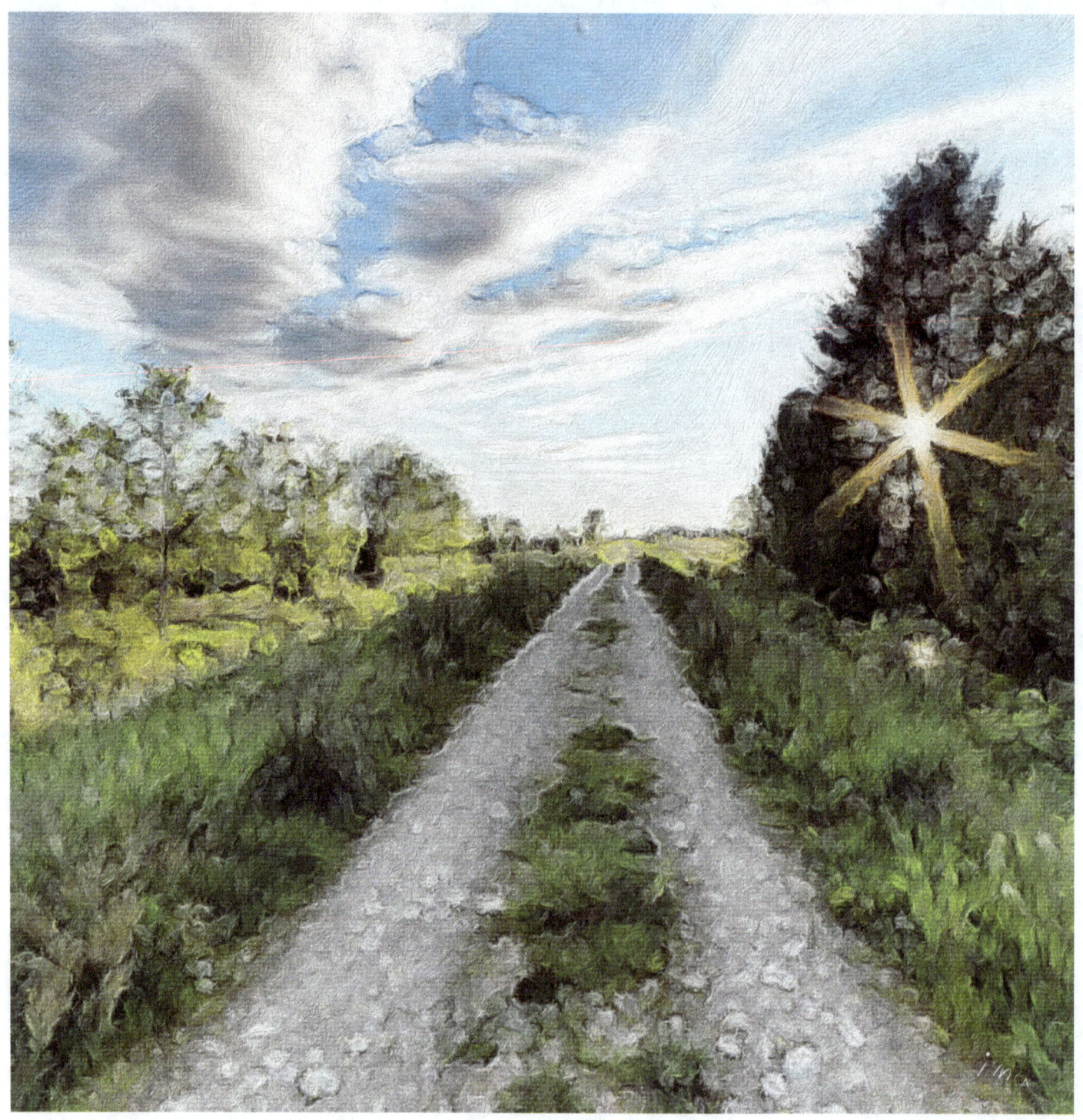

This Sacred Summer web prepares the kindness found on the Summer holiday's dusty road.

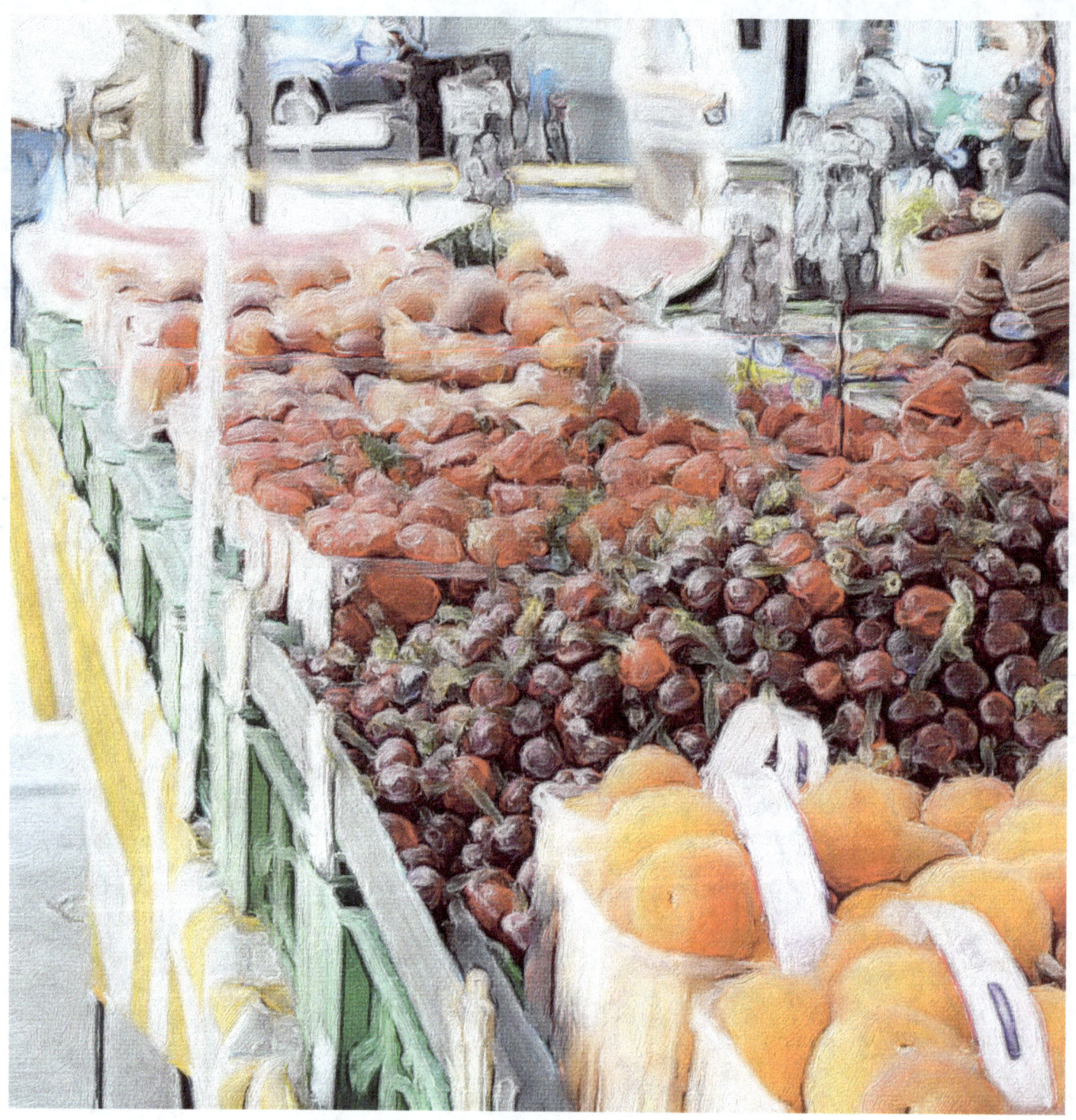

Eager to visit farmers' stands and county fairs
to savor and appreciate edible botanicals grown,
by this sincere and kind rhythmic code.

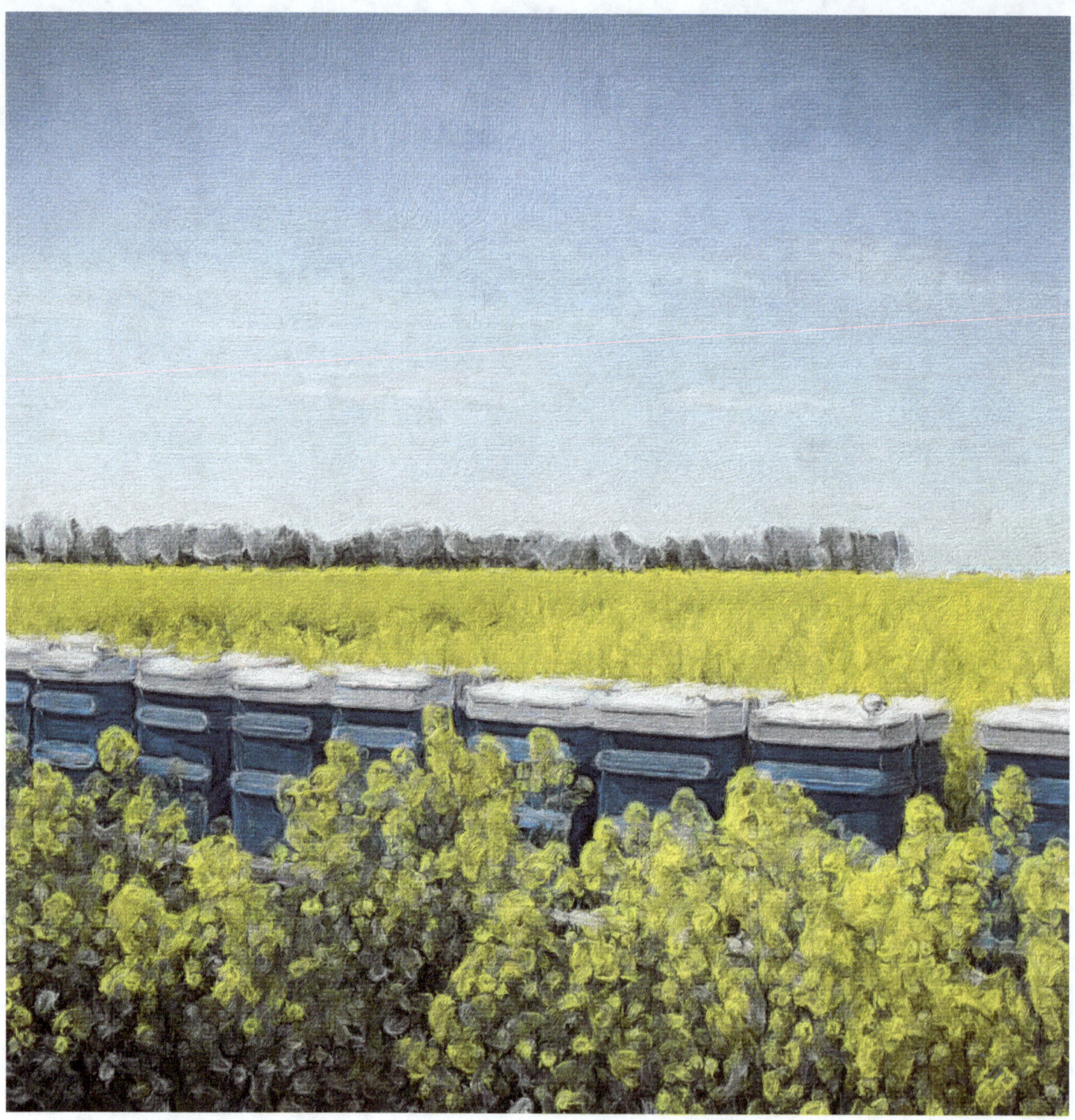

Not to ignore the honey bees' request to provide water twain from fields and gardens to beehives, their nests.

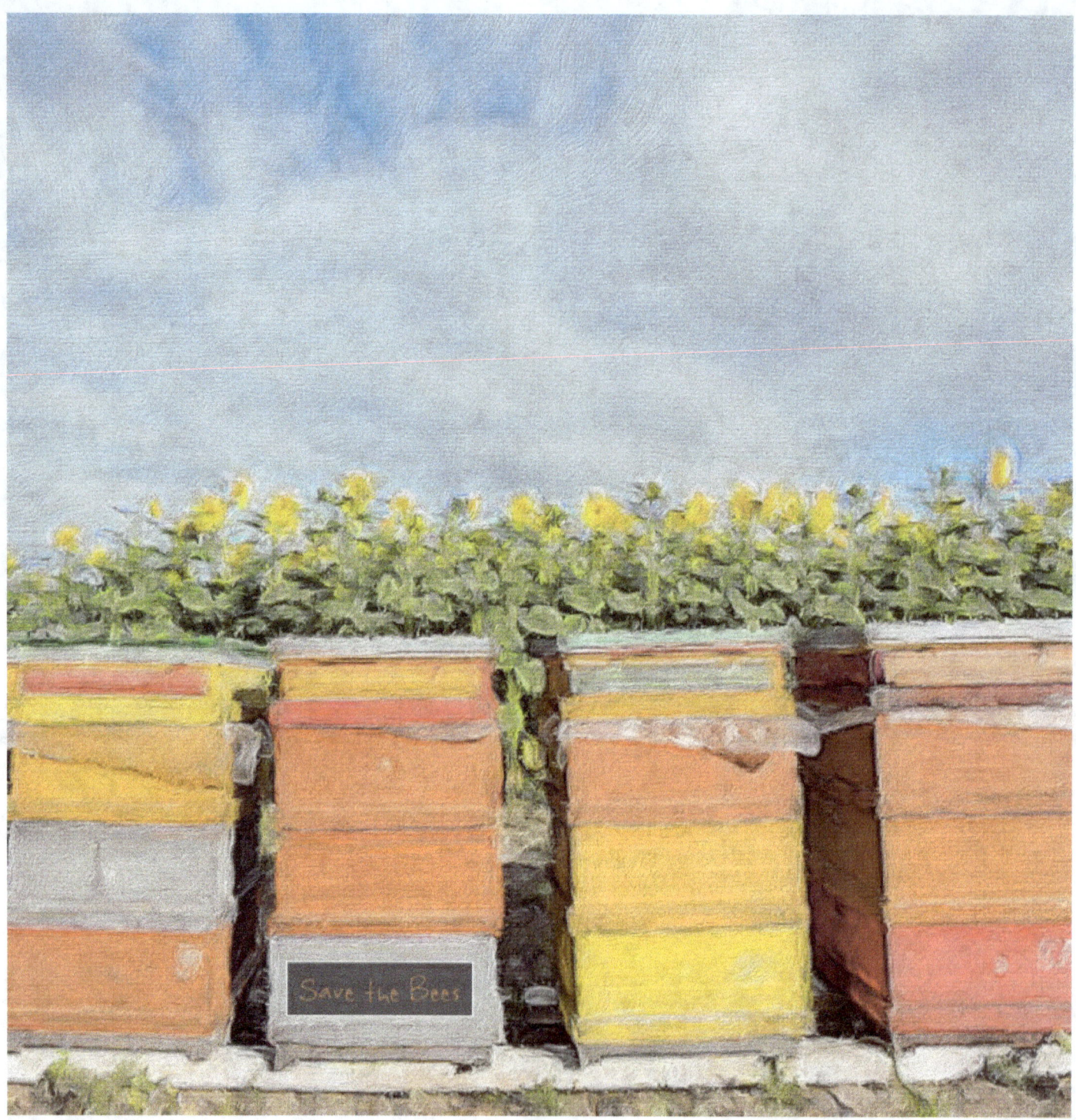

Summer's need for shallow water troughs (for tender pollinators) should every heat-temper season be addressed.

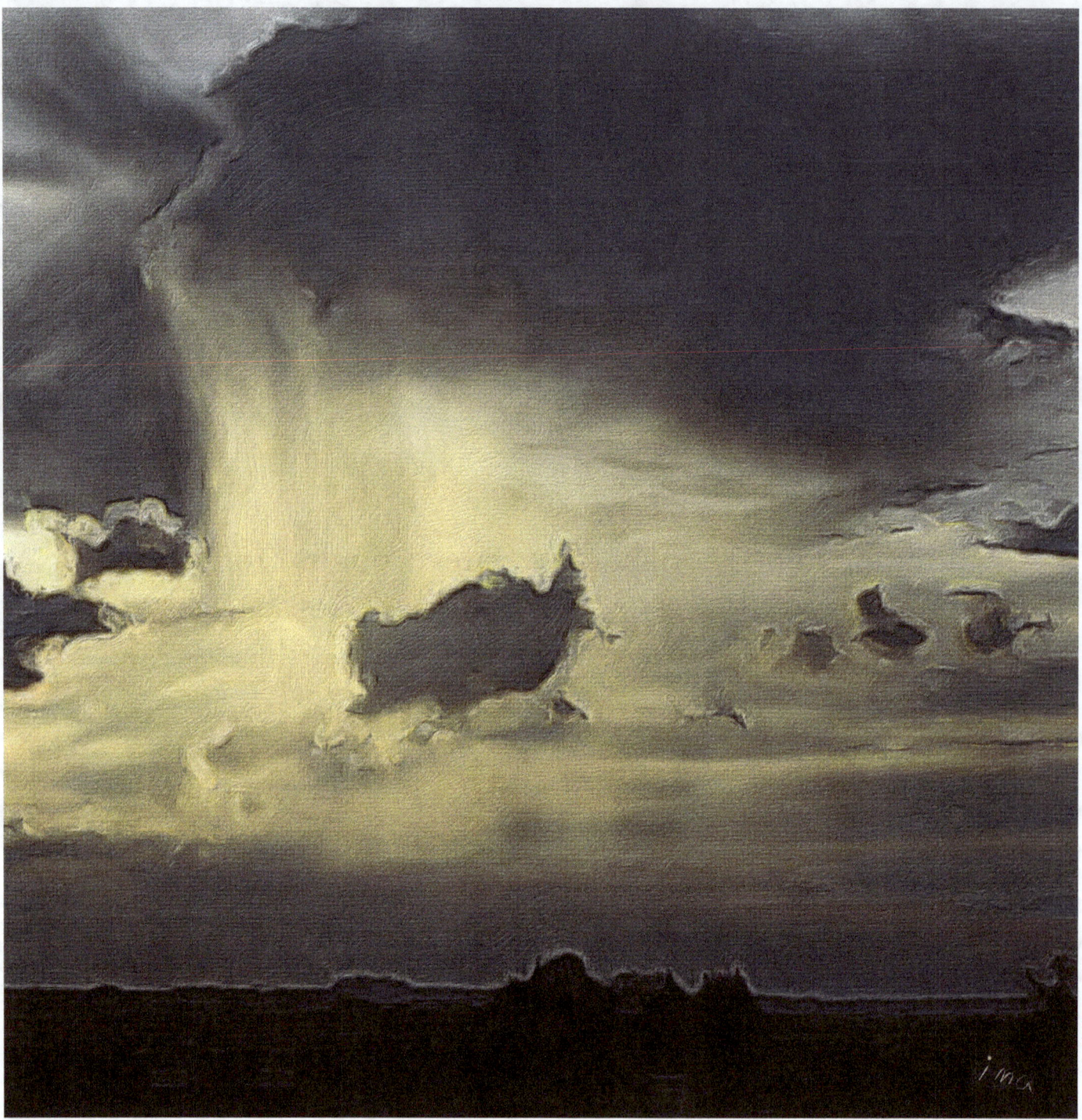

I am not at odds with being warm; liken it a solid faith.
Yet, can positively be in prayer, for the rain to find the dust,
enjoy the petrichor experience, and celebrate the rain's bathe.

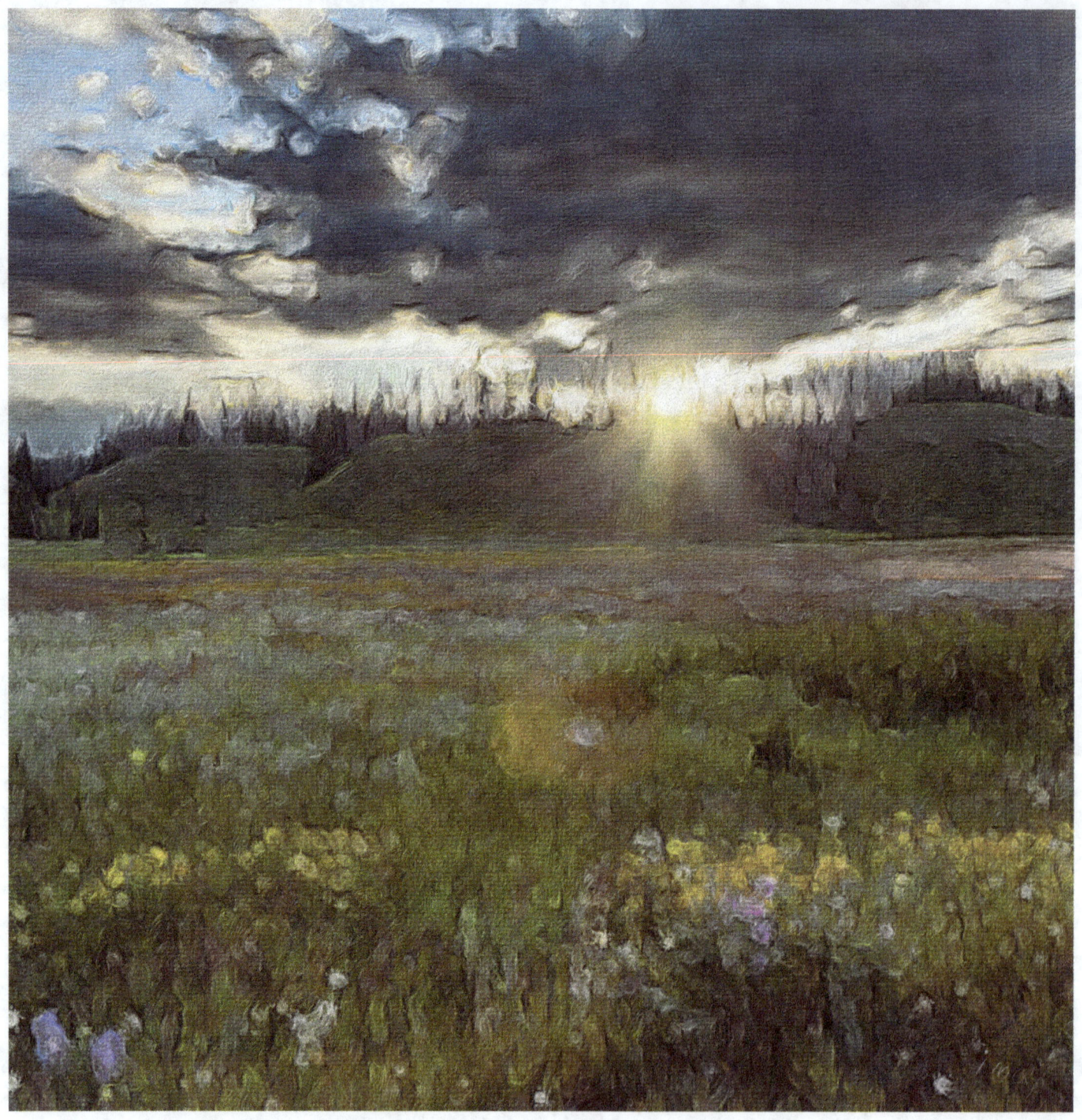

That anticipated inclination, the visits to parks,
is a genuine impulse to witness God's splendor,
those natural wonders - more than just a "bucket list."

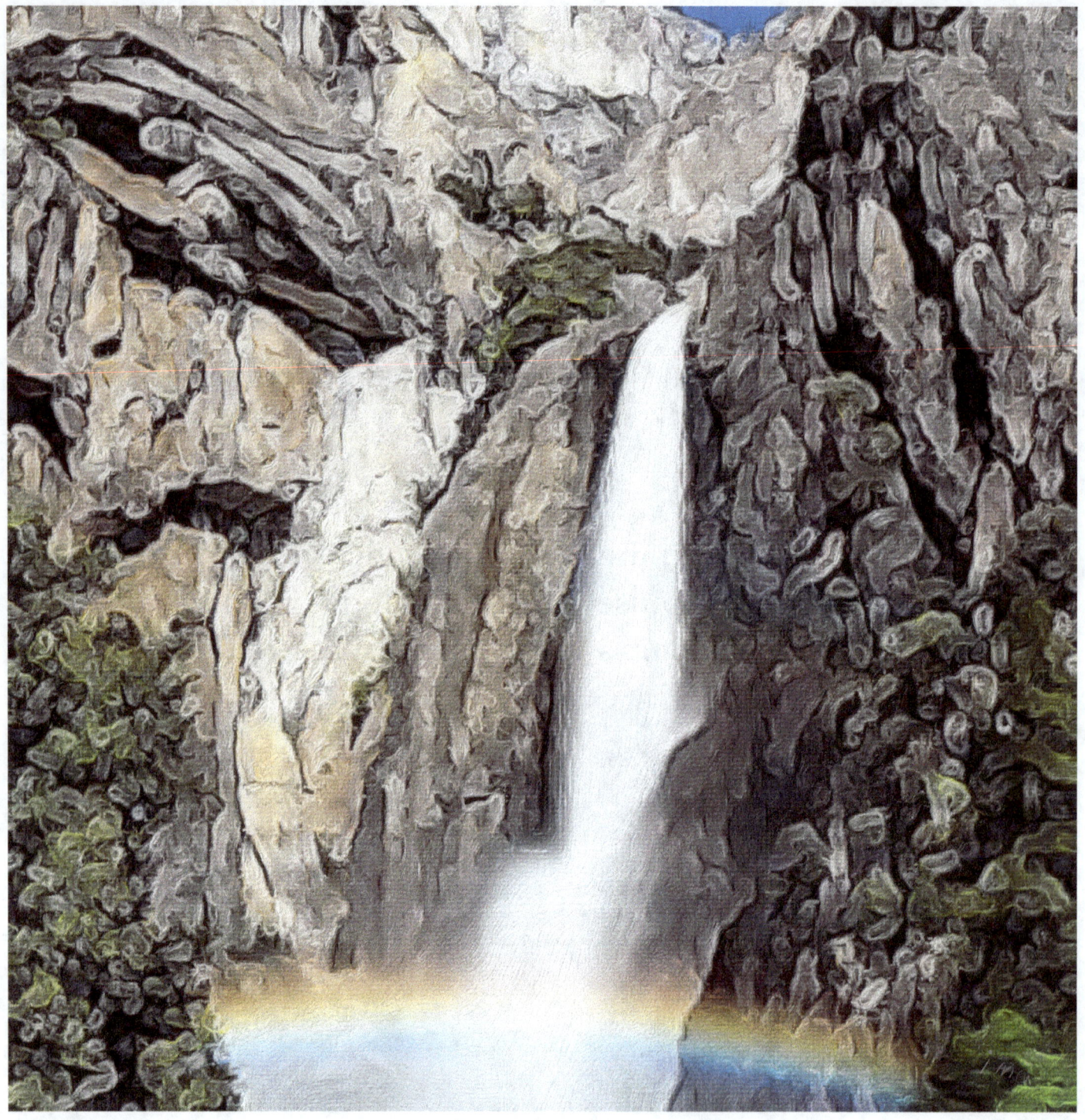

Our combined goal as a preservation "holy grail" is for the Sacred Summer season with all profound gifts brought by the Sun to perpetually exist.

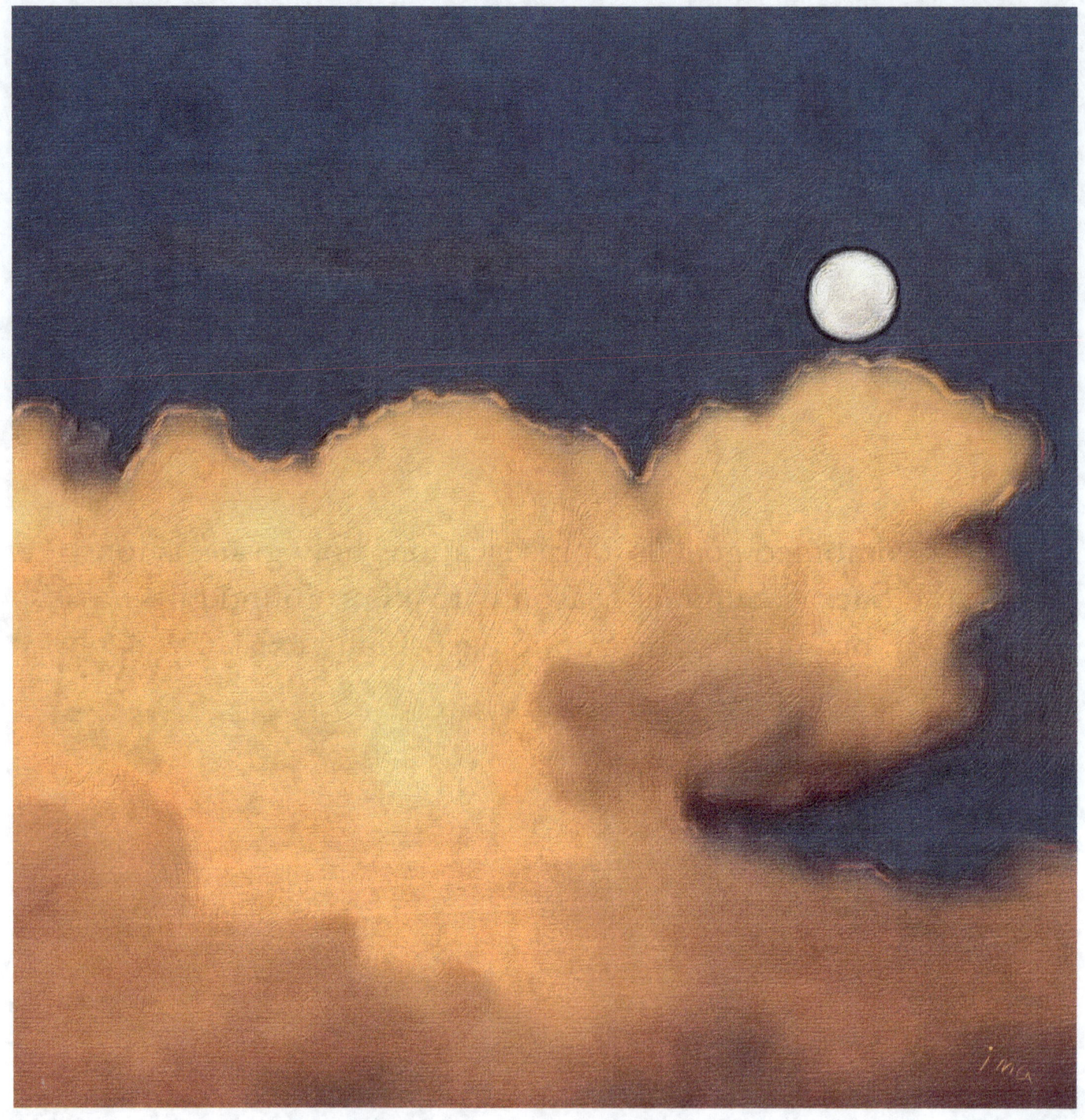

Sacred Summer

The Sacred Summer Sun, on the solstice, ends our lingering saisonnière lunar chill woes.
Bringing warmth throughout the essential cores, even down to roots and toes.
This ray of warmth forever increases through about three, and quelques jours, glorious months.
Forever gaining traction with this calm, curing, solacing, and earnestness punch.
Like all seasons, the start of Summer's temper is somewhere in the mid-middle.
Encouraging our wall calendar's solstice schedule to be very civil.
Marking the Summer Solstice Day divine and to all acknowledged... Hear Ye! Hear Ye! Sacred.
Improving every day on Divine Spring and what that season's growth created.
This eagerness for sincere Summer warmth has deep, tender roots.
Growing in these temps très chaud, a pearl of courageous wisdom shares the youthful fortitude already introduced..
Hark to these altrical/precocial births that began with Divine Spring.
Sacred Summer speeds forth la croissance des plantes germination upswing.
Thriving deciduous growth encourages spheres of joy.
Reassured conifers relax and increase their ever-flourishing voice.
our Summer Sunbeams
are forever nourishing...
sacred sustenance
The advance of Sacred Summer months thrives on retrieving generational wisdom.
And welcomes the same, God's wise animal kingdom.
Are you, are you like I, eager for fields of sunflowers?
These welcoming mirrors mimic all her sunshowers.
And indeed, note that the sacred butterflies increase our crops.
The Sacred Summer seasonal rotation changes the rhythmic clocks.
Sending mullers in contemplation to glorious and spectacular beaches.
The latish setting Sun highlights a delightful find - those precious flying creatures.
Fields of grain grow strong within, do promise of goodwill bread.
The sacred Sun, to its core, her rays are the land-to-farmer's goodness thread.
This Sacred Summer web prepares the kindness found on the Summer holiday's dusty road.
Eager to visit farmers' stands and county fairs to savor and appreciate
edible botanicals grown by this sincere and kind rhythmic code.
Not to ignore the honey bees' request to provide water twain from fields and gardens to beehives, their nests.
Summer's need for shallow water troughs (for tender pollinators) should every heat-tempered season be addressed.
I am not at odds with being warm; liken it to a solid faith.
Yet, can positively be in prayer for rain to find the dust, enjoy the petrichor experience, and celebrate the rain's bathe.
That anticipated inclination, the visit to parks, is a genuine impulse to witness
God's splendor, those natural wonders - more than just a "bucket list."
Our combined goal as a preservation "holy grail" is for the Sacred Summer
season with all profound gifts brought by the Sun to perpetually exist.
Isabelle Athmann